D1089225

COVER PHOTO: Detail of the Glory and of one column of the baldachin

BACK OF COVER: Detail of a putto on one of the four bronze columns of the baldachin.

TRANSLATION FROM THE ITALIAN BY: Johnn Lipford

DRAWNS: Angela Foschini

St. Peter's dome, seen at sunset from the Pincian Hill. A view whose like exist nowere else in the world. ▷

© 2001. FUTURA EDIZIONI
IV Reprinting 2006

e-mail: futured@tiscali.it

00156 ROMA - Via Costantino Mortati, 130
Tel. 06/41218931

All rights reserved.
No parts of this book may be reproduced
in any form without permission in writing
from the publisher.

St. Peter's

Basilica

Art and Light

PHOTOGRAPHS AND TEXT BY GIANFRANCO CRIMI

HISTORY OF ST. PETER'S BASILICA

In July 64 BC a great fire destroyed entire quarters of Rome. It hadn't been desired by the emperor Nero, but he did take advantage of it to make substantial modifications to the city's fabric. These created such discontent in the population that they believed the emperor responsible for the fire. He, to divert suspicion from himself, gave the blame for it to the Christians, a new religious sect that was not as yet very well known.

Thus began a ferocious persecution, during which the apostle Peter, along with many others, was martyred. The site of his martyrdom was Caligula's circus, near by the Vatican hill, and he was buried in a graveyard in the area. Archaeological digs made beneath the basilica from 1939 to 1950 brought to light a necropolis dating to the second century BC. Here too was found a tomb consisting of two aediculas one atop the other, backed up against a red-plastered wall, made of bricks bearing imperial seals dating to around 160 AD.

Probably owing to the expansion of the burial area, this wall was built to delimit a definite place, where people went to venerate that small monument.

After the red wall was built another wall, called "of the graffiti" was reared perpendicular to it, and on it was found a legend: Petr en, which in Greek, if a few letters canceled by time are added, would become Petros eni, that is "Peter is here".

Gaius, Roman priest at the time of pope Zephyrin (199-217), after a quarrel with a certain Proclus, a supporter of the Eastern Orthodox church and chief of the sect of the Cataphryges, asked this latter to follow him to the Vatican hill area and then along the Via Ostiense, to show him the tombs of the two apostles, which he called "the trophies". By this Gaius shows that around 200 AD the Romans were venerating the two tombs in the same places as they are found today. This area was thrown into considerable confusion when the emperor Constantine, after his victory over Maxentius at the Milvian bridge, gave the start up to construction work on the basilica. Pope Sylvester I and the emperor acknowledged that small monument to be the tomb of the apostle Peter. Otherwise, nothing could explain the enormous excavation work, the considerable expense sustained, and all the difficulties involved to erect the basilica right on that spot.

The ancient basilica was preceded by a staircase and by an arcaded court, called the *Atrio Paradiso*, having in its center a fountain in the form of a large bronze pinecone, which currently stands in the court of the same name in the Vatican. It had five entrance doors and its interior consisted of a nave and four aisles, delimited by four files of 22 columns. Peter's tomb could be viewed up until the times of pope Gregory the Great (590-604), when the flooring was raised and an altar was placed on the tomb. The ceiling was made of wood. Over the centuries it underwent sackings, owing to the barbarian invasions and the abandonment of Rome by the papacy, when it was transferred to Avignon. Artists such as Giotto, Pietro Cavallini and Filarete contributed to its decoration and furnishings.

Pope Nicholas V (1447-1455), after having an expert inspection made by Leon Battista Alberti, decided to build a new church, one more in line with the new Rennaissance tastes, and assigned the design to Alberti and to his disciple Bernardo Rossellino. But the work was presently interrupted by the pope's death.

n 1505 Julius II took back up the idea of building a completely new church, thinking more than anything else of his own mausoleum, which, according to a design by Michael Angelo, was to be composed of some forty statues. The pope, thinking that competition would sharpen their invention, awarded the commission for the design of the new basilica both to Giuliano da Sangallo and to Donato Bramante. He chose the latter's design, which envisaged a church with a Greek cross plan, which was the more grandiose and perhaps also more in line with his own ambitious project. Work started up on April 18th 1506. Vasari relates that the tombs of popes, paintings, mosaics and many very fine decorations were lost in the process. Only St. Peter's altar was saved, and the old tribune. The pope's death in 1513, and Bramante's the next year, brought about the end of the work.

Leo X (1513-1521) awarded the commission to Giuliano da Sangallo and assigned as technical experts to work with him Raphael and fra Giocondo da Verona.

The new design was a Latin cross and would involve an enormous sum to realize. This led the pope to withhold execution of the plan; furthermore, those he had commissioned all died, the last in 1520 being Raphael, at just 37 years of age.

In 1527 Roma was sacked by Charles V's German mercenaries. After this long pause, Siena architect Baldassarre Peruzzi was called on, he presenting a number of designs that were never concretely realized.

There then followed Antonio da Sangallo, Giuliano's grandson, called by Paul III, who, as the documents of the *Reverenda Fabbrica* show, was the main architect from 1528 through 1546, the year in which he died. But even here nothing substantial was accomplished.

At this point pope Paul III decided to call in the by now seventy-year-old Michael Angelo to accept the commission as chief architect of the "Reverend Building", which, after various hesitations, he accepted, receiving his commission on January first 1547. The compensation that the pope had established was one hunded gold *scudi* per month. But Michael Angelo did not accept any recompense, and thus he was the donor of no less than 30,600 *scudi*: the richest gift a private party had ever made.

Michael Angelo gave a considerable impulse to the work and presented a wooden model of the dome – it can still be seen in the Reverend Building – which itself needed a good three years of work and an expenditure of 5660 *scudi*. When Michael Angelo died in 1564, the work had reached the drum of the dome and the spaces for the four corner chapels had been completed.

In that same year Pirro Ligorio was appointed, he being aided by Jacopo Barozzi, called Il Vignola. But Pius V's discontent with the design led to Ligorio's being sent away. The work went ahead without taking on the main problem - the construction of the dome - which was completed only in 1590 by Giacomo Della Porta. In this regard, a source in the archives states: "Monday May 19th 1590; a solemn mass was sung by a canon and the last stone was set in the dome, accompanied by great merriment and salvos from the papal artillery". In 1593 the construction of the lantern was finished, the cross then being placed on its summit.

In 1605 Paul V published a call for bids on the new facade, and at once started off the demolition of the parts still standing of the old basilica. Thus were lost the splendid mosaics of the oratory of John VII, the thirteenth-century frescoes, the famous atrium, and numerous art treasures.

Carlo Maderno (1556-1629) was awarded the job and on November 5th 1607 the foundations of the facade were laid. Paul V took council with a special Cardinals' Congregation, which had been appointed some time before, to reach a definitive decision as to the plan the basilica should have. The decision was to definitively forsake the Greek cross for the Latin, with the addition of three chapels per side.

This decision however implied a false note in the architectural design, something that Michael Angelo had been afraid of when he wrote that Bramante's design must not be veered from.

In any event, it was preferred in order to permit processional ceremonies inside the church, as well as to be able to build a baptistry and a sacristy and to permit the incorporation of the *Loggia delle Benedizioni*.

Maderno's work went ahead up to 1612, and gave the basilica the form that we currently see.

On Maderno's death Urban VIII (1623-1644) appointed as new architect and director of works Gian Lorenzo Bernini (1598-1680), who was followed by Carlo Fontana (1634 -1714), appointed on March 30th 1697.

With Bernini the great work of the improvement and furnishing of the basilica and of the square before it was finished. In the eighteenth century the basilica's most serious problem was the cracks discovered in the dome, and Luigi Vanvitelli was appointed to superintend the repair work.

ST PETER'S SQUARE

It was Alexander VII (1655-1667) who decided upon the construction of the square, especially to permit the crowds of faithful to assist at the most solemn functions. In particular, the feast of *Corpus Domini*, which at the time was taken much to heart.

St. Peter's square is in fact a huge ellipse, formed by seventeen meter wide colonnade made up of 284 columns in ranks of four and of 88 travertine pilasters. Its enwrapping form, with its definite allegorical intention, is thus explained by Bernini: "since St. Peter's church is almost the mother of all the others, it had to have a portico that would show how it receives, with open arms, maternally, Catholics, to confirm them in their belief; and heretics, to reunite them to the church, and infidels, to enlighten them in the new faith". The two straight arms, each 120 meters long, have names: the one to the left is *Charlemagne*, and the one to the right, *Constantine*. It is through this latter, through the grand staircase, that access is had to the Vatican Palace. Under Clement XI (1700-1721) the 140 statues atop the colonnade were placed. They depict the defenders of the faith, the founders of religious orders, popes, bishops, Doctors of the church, saints and martyrs. Gian Lorenzo Bernini improved the square itself by adding to Maderno's original fountain, the one to the right, another almost identical, symmetrically with respect to the obelisk. The obelisk is 25 meters tall, and is fashioned from a single block of red granite. It is the only one in Rome that has no hieroglypihc inscriptions. It was transported from Heliopolis, Egypt, by the emperor Caligula and placed in the circus he had built in the Vatican area, where a considerable number of Christians and the apostle Peter himself were killed. It remained there up until 1586, when at Sixtus V's behest it was placed in its present position. This technically difficult enterprise was conducted by Domenico Fontana, with the aid of his brother Giovanni. It took four months and involved the employment of a thousand men, of 4000 pounds of jute and iron, of 130 horses, and of 44 winches. On its top are heraldic elements referring to Alexander VII: the mountains and the stars; at its base are lions, Sixtus V's heraldic motif; and the eagles are the symbol of the Conti family, from which Innocent XIII came.

Between the obelisk and the fountains are two porphyry disks that indicate the focuses of the elipse, from either of which the precise alignment of the four files of columns can be observed. The four light standards were placed by Pius IX (1846-1878). To be noted on the cobblestone pavement too are the marble tondos, with the wind rose. The statues of saints Peter and Paul, sculpted by G. de Fabris and A. Tadolini, were placed in 1847, also by Pius IX.

THE FACADE

The facade, with the 34 steps leading up to it, is the work of Carlo Maderno. It is 45.50 meters tall and 117 meters long, and is scanned by eight gigantic columns 27 meters tall and by four Corinthian style pilaster strips that support the cornice.

Above, on the balustrade, there are thirteen statues depicting Christ the Redeemer, St. John Baptist, and eleven apostles. At the sides the two eighteenth-century clocks, built by Giuseppe Valadier, have a distinguishing feature: the one to the left gives the mean time in Europe, and the one to the right the solar time. The center is dominated by the *Loggia delle Benedizioni* ("of the Blessings") from which the election of a new pope is announced, and from which too the *Urbi et Orbi* blessing is given to the city and to the world, at Christmas and Easter time. Below the tympanum, the *Consignment of the Keys* by Ambrogio Buonvicino (1552-1622).

THE ATRIUM

Five gates lead to the atrium; in the central gate can be seen the arms of Paul V; in the middle gates, those of Urban VIII, and in the two end gates, those of Pius VI.

In the atrium, the work of Carlo Maderno, the vault is decorated with stuccoes he designed, but executed by Buonvicino. To the sides of the lunettes are depicted the canonized popes, attributed to Luigi Ottoni and dating to 1719. To the left the equestrian statue of the emperor Charlemagne, by Augustino Cornacchini (1686-1754), executed in 1725.

On the opposite side, another equestrian statue depicting the Roman emperor Constantine, started by Bernini in 1654 and finished in 1670. To be noted are the cherubims placed over the portals, executed by Borromini, at the time a young stone-cutter in the service of his uncle Carlo Maderno.

Above, with its back to the central door, the Navicella mosaic, commissioned to Giotto by cardinal Jacopo Stefaneschi in 1298. What is seen now is a seventeenth-century copy. Only fragments exist of the original, depicting two angels, and these are found in the Vatican Museums.

The flooring was designed by Bernini and redone in 1880. The central part, which bears the symbol of John XXIII, was redone to commemorate the inauguration of Vatican Council II, on October 11th 1962.

THE DOORS

Of the basilica's five doors the oldest is the middle one, commissioned by pope Eugene IV to Antonio Averulino, called Il *Filarete* (1400-1469), which in Greek means friend of virtue. The first panels above represent Christ the Saviour and the Virgin; then come St. Paul with a sword and St. Peter who consigns the keys to a kneeling pope Eugene IV. Below, the judgement and beheading of St. Paul, the saint appearing to Plautillus, and the crucifixion of St. Peter.

Among the panels there are scenes depicting episodes from Eugene IV's papacy. He was the one who wished to outfit Constantine's basilica with bronze doors, because when he was in Florence he had admired the door of the baptistry, built by Lorenzo Ghiberti, in whose workshop Il Filarete worked. In the rear part there is the author's bizarre signature: the maestro astride a mule, followed by a merry company of helpers and disciples.

The first door to the left, called the "door of death" because funeral cortèges issued from it, is by Giacomo Manzu (1908-1991), who executed it between 1961 and 1964, on commission by John XXIII, who is also depicted on it. In it the artist takes on the theme of death with moving simplicity. On its rear is shown the entrance of the cardinals who took part in Vatican Couincil II.

The second door, called "of Good and Evil", by Luciano Minguzzi, was executed between 1970 and 1977.

The fourth, "of the Sacraments", is the work of Venanzio Crocetti.

And the last, the *Holy Door*, by Vico Consorti, was placed in 1949 to replace the old wood leaves, which went back to the eighteenth century.

Its sixteen recessed panels develop the theme of salvation.

Sant'Angelo bridge and the basilica, lighted.

The dome framed between the statues of saints Peter and Paul, from the start of Sant'Angelo bridge.

On the following page, the statue of St. Chatrine from Siena with the dome in the background.
The sun filtering through the colonnade at sunset.

On the preceding page, St. Peter's square in the first light of dawn.

Detail of the colonnade.

The bas-relief depicting the consignment of the keys to the apostle Peter, by Ambrogio Buonvicino, was placed by Paul V below the Loggia of the Blessings.

Detail of Bernini's fountain, to the left of the square. The sculptured arms are those of Clement X.

Detail of Maderno's fountain. The sculptured arms are those of Paul V.

Detail of the statue of St. Peter by Giuseppe de Fabris.

The statue of St. Paul, by Adamo Tadolini. In the background the clock, by Giuseppe Valadier, that indicates the mean European time.

The minor domes of the Gregorian chapel, to the right, and of the Clementine chapel, to the left, which flank the Cupolone, or "big dome".

At the base of the dome a bust of Michael Angelo was placed.

On the following page, the statue of Christ making a blessing gesture,
with in the background the small lantern and the ball.

▷

One of the two clocks by Giuseppe Valadier, placed by Pius VI in 1789. it indicating the time in Italy.
Below it there is the huge bell of St. Peter's, weighing 9000 kilograms, which is rung at Christmas, at
Easter, for the feast of Saints Peter and Paul. and every time the *Urbi et Orbi* blessing is pronounced.

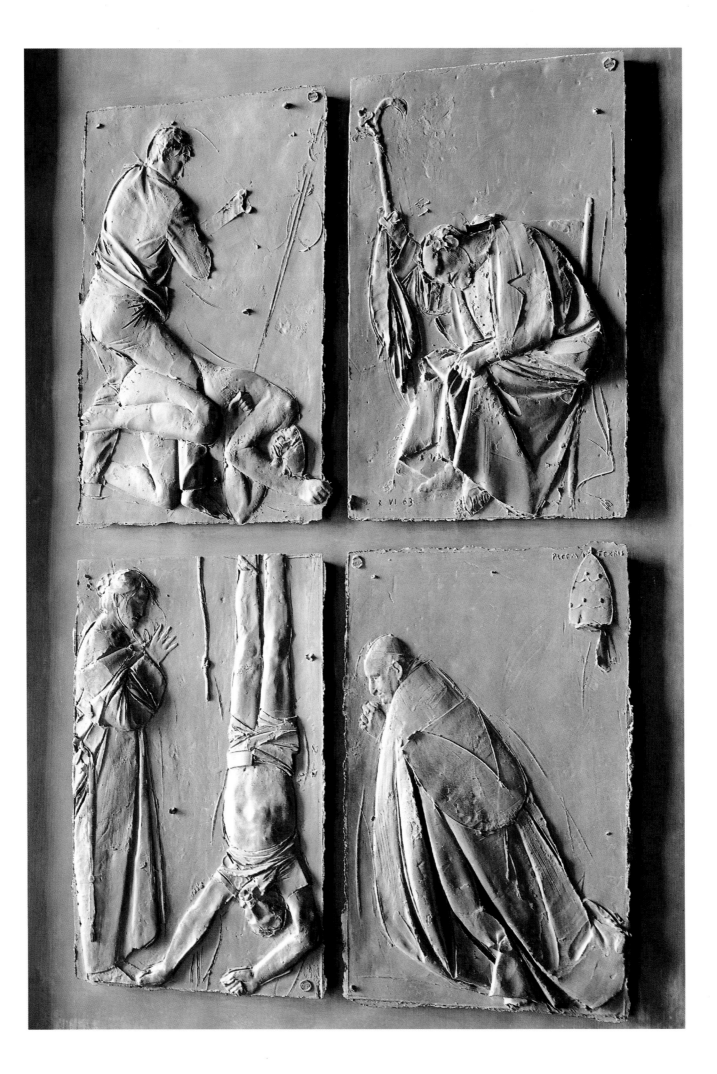

Detail of the door of
Death

Detail of the door of
Good and Evil

The basilica's oldest door, built by Antonio Averulino, called Il Filarete.
St. Peter consigning the keys to pope Eugene IV.

The judgement and beheading of St. Paul.

Crucifixion of St. Peter.

The sculptor's bizarre signature: the maestro astride a mule preceded by a merry company of aides and disciples.

The Holy Door, by Vico Consorti. Hung in 1949 to replace the old eighteenth-century door.
The theme of salvation is developed in its sixteen panels.

Jesus promising salvation to the thief on the cross, who invokes it

Jesus throws Paul from his horse.

On the preceding page, view of the nave.

The two holy water fonts at once give an idea of the proportions of the basilica, since they are a good two meters high. They were executed in 1725 by Agostino Cornacchini, Francesco Moderati, Giuseppe Lironi and Giovan Battista De Rossi.

Detail of a putto of the left holy water font.

The marble decoration of the lower parts of the columns was begun under Gregory XIII, continued under other popes, and was finished by Bernini under a commission granted him by Innocent X.
In this tondo we see the dove, which forms part of the pope's arms.

Pairs of putti support sculptured medallions containing the effigies of the first fifty-six martyred popes; others support ovals with tiaras and keys, symbols of the papacy. The dove is the heraldic symbol of Innocent X.

One of the twenty-eight allegorical statues depicting the Virtues, sculpted by Bernini's co-workers. In the background, an angel of the dome of St. Sebastian.

The ceiling and gilt stuccoes with the arms of Pius VI.

The statues depicting the Virtues: *Faith*.

Starting in 1700, the statues of saints who had founded religious orders and congregations were placed in the Basilica. Shown is a detail of St. Peter of Alcantara, by Francesco Vergara y Bartual (1753).

View of the nave, with in its center the bronze baldachin by Gian Lorenzo Bernini.

The Confession, built on the vertical over St. Peter's tomb, is delimited by a marble balustrade where eighty-nine flames burn eternally in gilt bronze cornucopias, which were designed by Mattia De Rossi. Two ramps lead to the room richly decorated with marbles, with at its center a bronze railing holding two statues, of St. Peter and of St. Paul.

The papal altar, consecrated by Clement VIII in 1594, surmounted by the imposing bronze baldachin by Bernini, who worked on it from 1624 to 1633, commissioned by Urban VIII. The marble column bases bear in their centers the symbol of the pope, the Barberini bees, and there is also sculpted a sequence depicting the various phases of the birth. They were executed by Radi and Castelli, the latter better known as Borromini, whose sound technical contribution to the execution of the monument has been justly acknowledged.

The ninth-century mosaic depicts the Saviour. It is the only element of the old basilica that is still to be found in its same place. The silver casket, work of Roman silversmiths of the 18th century, was a gift of Benedict XIV. It contains the *palli*, which are stoles woven of the wool of lambs blessed on the day of the feast of St. Agnes, and each year he makes a present of them to a few archbishop-metropolitans.

The crucifix on the papal altar. Alexander VII commissioned Bernini to make new crucifixes and candelabras for the various altars in the Basilica. He designed them and had them executed by Ercole Ferrata.

The columns are ornamented with leafy branches and small putti who are chasing the bees, symbol of the Barberini family. The baldachin is 29 meters high, as high as Palazzo Farnese, and weighs a total 93 tons, of which only 62 is metal, since its interior consists of mortar.

Detail of one of the columns of the baldachin. In the background the balcony of the column of St. Helena.

On the preceding pages, putti holding up the keys and the tiara, symbols of the papacy.

A sunbeam lights up the cross placed at the top of the baldachin.

The blessing gesture unites these three images: The first depicts the statue of Pius XII, work of Francesco Messina, executed in 1964. The other portrays Pius XI, a work executed by Francesco Nagni in 1949.

The bronze statue of St. Peter was attributed to Arnolfo di Cambio (1245-1310), and careful study of its construction technique and of the alloy of metals used has confirmed a dating compatible with the techniques of the time. The veneration the statue enjoys is shown by the way the toes of the foot are consumed, they being kissed or caressed by the faithful.

The cartoons for the mosaics of the evangelists, in the tondi placed at the four corners of the columns, were furnished by Giovanni De Vecchi of Borgo San Sepolcro, a painter and mosaicist, who executed the *St. John*, with the eagle, and the *St. Luke*, with the angel. The *St. Mark*, with the lion, and the *St. Matthew*, with the ox, were executed by mosaicist Marcello Provenzale to cartoons by Cesare Nebbia.

The angels placed at the top of the baldachin are the work of François Duquesnoy.

On the following page, a view of the interior of the dome
and of the transept.

The internal decoration of the dome, in stucco and mosaic, was commissioned by Clement VIII (1529–1605) to the Knight of Arpino (Giuseppe Cesari, 1568-1640).
Starting from the outside, we see depicted: beshops, Christ, the Virgin Mary, St. John Baptist, the Apostles, angels and cherubims and, on the interior of the lantern, God.

On the following pages, the piers, started by Bramante and brought to a finish by Michael Angelo, are 45 meters high, and their diameter is almost 71 meters. To make a comparison, the plan of the church of San Carlino alle Quattro Fontane by Borromini could be placed in the area of one pier.
Urban VIII (1623-1644), encharged Bernini to decorate the piers. The artist designed four loggias with round arches, with bas-reliefs inspired by relics and framed by tendril columns. Below, in marble-lined niches, he placed the statues, each five meters tall, of St. Helena, St. Longines, St. Andrew and Veronica.

The *Veronica* is the work of Francesco Mochi (1580-1654).

St. Helena, the emperor Constantine's mother, was sculpted by Andrea Bogli in 1646.

The statue of Longines, the Roman soldier who pierced Jesus's side with his lance, was sculpted by Bernini.

The statue of St. Andrew is by François Duquesnoy (1594-1643). In the foreground, the base of a column of the baldachin sculpted by Radi and by Borromini, at the time a young stonemason in the suite of his uncle, Carlo Maderno.

The chapel of the Pietà still conserves the famous marble group sculpted by the twenty-five-year-old Michael Angelo, for cardinal Jean Bilhiéres de Lagraulas, Charles VIII's ambassador to pope Alexander VI. It was moved a number of times until it found its current location here in 1749. Its eliptical marble base is the work of Borromini. This is the only statue that Michael Angelo placed his signature on: it is on the belt that crosses the breast of the Madonna, because there were (false) rumors that it had been sculpted by Cristoforo Solari. Departing from iconographic tradition, Michael Angelo portrayed the Madonna with a youthful face, because, some have it, having lost his own mother as a child he sought to idealize her features.

The monument to Innocent XII, by Francesco Della Valle and Ferdinando Fuga, 1746.
In the foreground the allegory of *Justice*, and to the left, *Charity*.

The chapel of the Holy Sacrament is preceded by the elegant Baroque railing by Borromini (1599-1667).
The stucco decorations of the vault, which depict episodes from the Old and New Testaments,
owe to Giacomo Perugino to designs by Pietro da Cortona; his is also the altar-piece,
depicting the Trinity, the basilica's only tapestry, since from 1626 on the altar-pieces began
to be transposed into mosaics, to save them, as had happened for some,
from irremediable deterioration.

Bernini's tabernacle with two angels in prayer at its sides, who drew inspiration from Bramante's little temple in the church of San Pietro in Montorio.

TWo of the sixteen angels that adorn the arches of the chapel.

St. Vincent de Paul, sculpted by Pietro Bracci (1700-1773).

Above, in the niches, are the statues of the saints who founded religious orders and congregations, placed there since 1700. Depicted here is Domenico Guzman, sculpted in 1706 by Pierre Legros.

St. Filippo Neri, by Giovan Battista Maini (1690-1752).

The funeral monument of Gregory XIII (1572 – 1585). To the left, an allegory of *Religion* holding in her hand the Bible, and in the other a tablet with the words: "I know His works and His faith". The other statue portrays *Strength*, with the features of Minerva, who is raising a drapery to show the bas-relief that commemorates the calendar reform, desired by this pope, which shifted October 4th on the earlier calendar (going back to Julius Caesar) to October 15th. The winged dragon is a symbol from the arms of the Boncompagni family. Camillo Rusconi (1658-1728) was the sculptor of this work.

Here we are in the Gregorian chapel, and brought to a conclusion by Giacomo della Porta. The altar of the *Madonna del Soccorso* (of Aid), with a wealth of marble decorations and its splendid African marble columns, is the work of Girolamo Muziano (1528-1592) It takes its name from the 11th-century fresco moved here by Gregorio XV on September 13th 1580.

The monument to Benedict XIV, Lambertini, with at the sides *Wisdom and Unselfishness*. The first two were sculpted by Pietro Bracci, who intoduced the innovation of portraying the pope not seated or in a contemplative attitude, but in the act of rising with his right hand making a blessing gesture.
The allegory of *Unselfishness* was sculpted by his pupil, Gaspare Sibilia.

Funeral monument of Clement XIII, the work of Antonio Canova ((1757 – 1822), who inroduced the Neoclassical style into St. Peter's. To the left is *Religion*, and to the right the *Genius of Death*, which is extinguishing the torch of life; at the foot are two travertine lions guarding the tomb. On the urn, in relief, the figures of *Charity and of Hope*.

Mattia De Rossi designed this monument to Clement X, sculpted by Ercole Ferrata, with at its sides Clemency, by Giuseppe Mazzuoli, and Beneficence, by Lazzaro Morelli. On the base is reproduced the opening of the Holy Door during the 1675 Jubilee, by Leonardo Reti.

St. Elia, founder of the Carmelite order, sculpted by Agostino Cornacchini (1686-1727).

Glory, by Bernini, which appears to be pointed to by St. Elia's arm, lighted by the sun.
The dove symbolizes the Holy Spirit.

The vault of the chapel Gregoriana, decorated during the first decades of the 18th century with stuccoes and mosaics, to designs by Niccolò Ricciolini.

Funeral monument of Urban VIII, Barberini, designed by Bernini in 1627 and brought to a conclusion in 1646. The statue is of bronze with gold highlights; above the sarcophagus Death is figured, which is writing the pope's name on a parchment. To the sides in white Carrara marble, Justice and Charity.
In the following pages, details of *Justice* and *Charity.*

The altar of the Throne, a work by Gian Lorenzo Bernini, in whose interior is enclosed an acacia wood chair with ivory decorations and oakwood inlays. According to an investigation made at the order of Paul VI in 1968, carried out by a special commission, the Chair goes back to the ninth century, and it is supposed that it was brought to Rome by Charles the Bald, when he was crowned in the basilica by John VIII, in 875. Alexander VII gave Bernini the commission of building a monument that would do justice to this ancient chair, and he conceived this "case" in the form of a throne. Its solemn placement took place on January 17th 1666. The statues to the sides, in gilt bronze, five meters tall, represent the Doctors of the Church. the two interior statues, St. Anastasius and St. Chrysostom, represent the Greek Church; the two outer ones, St. Ambrose and St. Augustine, the Latin Church.

Detail of the base of the Chair, with symbols of the arms of pope Alexander VII Chigi.

On the following page, St. Ambrose and St. Anastasius, St. Chrysostom and St. Augustine

The vault is decorated with stuccoes by Giovan Battista Maini, and their tondi represent *the consignment of the Keys*, the *crucifixion of Peter*, and *the beheading of the apostle Paul*.

◁

The monument to Paul III (1534-1549) erected at the desire of the college of cardinals, was conceived by Giacomo Della Porta (1533-1602). The starting design envisaged eight allegorical statues, but only four of them were built and of these, two ended up in Palazzo Farnese.
The statues depicted *Justice* and *Prudence*.

Detail of Bernini's *Glory*, in gilt stucco.

A sunbeam lights the apse.

St. Francis of Assisi, by Carlo Monaldi (1683-1760).

Giuliana Falconieri, by Paolo Campi (1670-1764).

The monument of Alexander VIII (1689-1691), to a design by Arrigo di San Martino, cast in bronze by Giuseppe Bertosi. The marble statues of *Religion* and of *Prudence* are the work of Angelo De Rossi. The bas-relief depicts a canonization of saints.

The altar of St. Leo Magnus (440-461) has a large bas-relief that was sculpted by Alessandro Algardi (1602-1656). It depicts the meeting of the pope with Attila, king of the Huns, whom he succeeded in stopping, thus saving Rome from destruction.

The chapel of the Madonna of the Column, takes its name from the image of the Virgin painted on a column of the old basilica. Paul VI honored it with the title of *Mater Ecclesiae*, and John Paul II had a mosaic copy of it placed on the outside wall of the Vatican palace.

Just behind are *Prudence* and *Justice*.

The monument of Alexander VII portrays the pope in prayer. Suddenly Death appears, with an hourglass in its hand, announcing the running out of the time of his life. In the foreground, the statues depicting *Charity*, with a child in arms, by Giuseppe Mazzuoli, and *Truth*, sculpted by Lazzaro Morelli and Giulio Cartari. Just behind are *Prudence* and *Justice*, by Giulio Cartari; their feet rest on England, where the pope had sought to block the borning Anglicanism. The pope's head was sculptured by Bernini. The gilt bronze skeleton was cast by G. Lucenti and its placement was a rather arduous task. The elegant draperies are in Sicilian jasper. The statues of *Truth* and of *Charity*, which at one time appeared with bare breasts, were covered up in 1833 at the behest of Innocent XI.

Detail of *Charity*.

Truth and *Justice*.

The vault of the chapel of St. Michele Arcangelo, begun by Michael Angelo and brought to a conclusion by Giacomo Della Porta.

Detail of the vault of the left transept, decorated by Vanvitelli with stuccoes executed by
Giovan Battista Maini.

St. Giovanni Di Dio, by Filippo della Valle (1698-1768).

St. Norbert, by Pietro Bracci.

The left ambulatory in foreshortened view. In the background the monument to Pius VII.

PIO · VIII · PONTIFICI · MAXIMO
IOSEPHVS · ALBANIVS · CARDINALIS

The monument to Pius VIII (1820-1823), a work by Pietro Tenerani (1789 – 1869).
A Neoclassicizing Roman sculptor, he was acquainted with the major sculptors who worked in Rome:
the Dane Thorvaldsen and Antonio Canova.
And he took his inspiration for this monument from *Canova's Clement XIII*.

The monument to Pius VII (1820-1823) by the Danish sculptor Bertel Thorvaldsen (1770-1844), who was living in Rome. To the sides two statues depicting the *Genius of Time* and the *Genius of History*; below, *Strength*, covered with a lion skin, and *Wisdom* with a book and an owl.

The monument to Leo XI, who reigned just twenty-seven days, conceived by Alessandro Algardi (1593-1654). Algardi also furnished the designs and sculpted the statue of the pope and the bas-relief on the urn. The statue of *Majesty* is by Ercole Ferrata. In the bas-relief is represented the abjuration of Calvinism performed by Henri IV, king of France. The statue of *Liberality*, which is pouring gold and jewels from a cornucopia, owes to Giuseppe Peroni.

The monument to Innocent XI (1676 - 1689) is the work of French sculptor Stefano Monnot, whose signature is on the shield; at its sides are allegories of *Faith* and of *Justice*. The bas-relief commemorates the defeat of the Turks at Vienna in 1683, the work of Giovanni Sobiesky. The overall design is by Carlo Maratta.

At the chapel of the Choir the basilica with nave and two aisles begins, according to Maderno's design. On the altar is depicted the Immaculate Virgin, surrounded by angels, St. Francis, St. Anthony of Padua and John Chrysostom, from the painting by Pietro Bianchi (1694 – 1740).

On December 8th 1854 Pius IX had the dogma of the Immaculate Conception proclaimed, and the image of the Madonna was crowned. Pius X placed on it a second crown of diamonds, donated by various countries, on the fiftieth anniversary of the proclamation of the dogma. Among the various artists taking part in the decoration of the chapel was Carlo Maratta (1625 – 1713). The elegant railing is the work of Borromini, who on September 9th 1628, signed a payment receipt for the first time with this name instead of his legal name, which was Francesco Castelli.

Detail of the stucco decorations and of the great Baroque organ dating to 1626

Detail of the *Immacolata.*

Detail of the decorations on the walls.

Detail of the stuccoes decorating the vault, executed by Giovan Battista Ricci da Novara, to designs by Giacomo della Porta.

A stucco angel in the chapel of the Choir.

The oldest funeral monument in the basilica, coming from the Constantinian basilica, dedicated to Innocent VIII, the work of Antonio Pollaiolo (1431-1498). The pope, depicted in the act of blessing, holds in his left hand the lance of Longines, a relic donated to him by Bajazet II. To the sides are represented the four cardinal Virtues: *Prudence*, *Justice*, *Strength* and *Temperance*. In the upper lunette, the theological Virtues: *Faith*, *Hope and Charity*. The original order envisaged the sarcophagus up above, on the brackets.

SANCTVS ALEXANDER

PIO PAPAE X

The bronze door with bas-reliefs illustrating moments in the papacy of St. Pius X.

Detail of the bronze reliefs.

◁

The monument to St. Pius X is by architect Florestano di Fasto, while the sculptured part was executed by Pier Enrico Astorri.

The monument to John XXIII is by Emilio Greco, and depicts the pope while he is visiting those imprisoned in Rome's Regina Coeli jail.

The monument to Maria Clementina Sobiesky, granddaughter of John II king of Poland; in 1719 she married James III Stuart, pretender to the throne of England.

The portrait of Maria Clementina Sobieski and the statue of *Charity* by Pietro Bracci.

The funeral stele of the monument to the Stuarts. It depicts James III, his son Charles III and cardinal Henry, Duke of York. The work was executed by Antonio Canova on commission by George III of England, holder of the throne the Stuarts claimed. The Stuart line became extinct in Rome, where its members had lived in exile.

The last chapel, that of the Baptistry, designed by Carlo Fontana (1634-1714), with in its center the red porphyry baptismal font. It was taken from an ancient monument and used as the cover for the sarcophagus of the emperor Otto III, who died in Rome in 983 and was entombed in the old basilica.
The gilt bronze cover is dominated by the Lamb of God and by the angels supporting the Holy Trinity, which is blessing the world. The altar-piece, the *Baptism of Jesus by John Baptist*, is a mosaic taken from a design by Carlo Maratta.